VIXEN

CHERENE SHERRARD

Autumn House Press
Pittsburgh

"Autumn House Press" and "Autumn House" are registered trademarks owned by Autumn House Press, a nonprofit corporation whose mission is the publication and promotion of poetry and other fine literature.

 Autumn House Press receives state arts funding support through a grant from the Pennsylvania Council on the Arts, a state agency funded by the Commonwealth of Pennsylvania, and the National Endowment for the Arts, a federal agency.

Cover art: "We Wear the Mask II," Krista Franklin, Collage on handmade paper, 2014. *Book & cover design:* Joel W. Coggins

ISBN: 978-1-938769-21-4
Library of Congress Control Number: 2017936010

For my parents,
Fredric and Martha Sherrard,
who never interrupted my stories.

CONTENTS

FOREST

THE SEDITIOUS SAGA OF ANNABELLE X AS TOLD TO THE ABOLITIONIST MRS. SARABETH CLARKE OF ROCHESTER, NEW YORK, IN NINE PARTS

what if,
then,
i had reared up baying,
and followed her off
into vixen country?

Lucille Clifton,
"one year later"

FOREST

LOVE IN THE TIME OF THE MACHETE

AFRICA IN CHAOS reads the headline of the Sunday paper.
I forget the name of the country but it doesn't matter.
They are all spiraling into disease, war, genocide.
And yet, Africa is *in* again.

Because fashion repeats there must have been another time
when it was a trendsetting continent. Perhaps twice
a century somebody peers through a telescope,
sees a child eating a cassava and exclaims: the new melon,
or spies a glitter in a cave and types: the new gemstone.

I too wish to be on everyone's tongue.
It means you are never far from hope or a handout.
But if Africa is in again, instead of documentaries
and truth and reconciliation hearings,
I want to see a romantic comedy.

Set in downtown Nairobi, Windhoek, or Cape Town.
A story about uncircumcised, educated lovers
who don't have AIDS, who vote, and at the end
don't emigrate to England. I want a happy ending
that maybe features a rhino but not one single pan
of an angry mob, women dancing, or men
drumming. The only white people I want to see
in this movie will be cab drivers or tourists.
No Dutch angles of an extra smoking in fatigues
stroking his AK-47 in the background,
while my couple dines at a boutique hotel,
before adjourning to an air-conditioned loft
for sex in the dark as Shakira plays on the radio.
No one will unload boxes of machetes
as if there were acres of sugar cane to cut.
There will be no helicopters, jungles,
or sand dunes (maybe the last scene has a sand dune)
but then only if my couple can ride into the sunset
in a Land Rover, after they shoot the rhino.

ONE MOMENT SHE WAS THERE AND THE NEXT

After The Good Shepherd (2006)

The award for best cinematography goes to:
her body buoyant above the bulbous jade
of the Congo
swarming with primates
                   some armed
others swinging their auburn limbs like Pollack
as they trapeze the trees. Above, her veil aerates,
a slim parachute, believe it will weave into
a net, that she will glide agile, land *en pointe*
in the clearing and not, please.
The camera tracks her acrobatics like a dream
from which you are desperate to wake, before.

Her hand brushes your cheek and it is wet, like the back of your neck
where your shirt clings—cast-off of a college coed
unnerved by the welts it drew across her torso.
As you dressed for this morning's business,
you never expected her to resemble your mother.
Her hand, sweaty, soft, sweeps across your upper lip
so like your mother's cool fingers when she left you
beneath the baobab for shade, or to get fufu,
you thought, in your greedy innocence.
Her head-cloth is indigo with white-white rings interlocking:
from the pattern, Mama Kuti could be your mother.

No camera or cell phone captured her descent: it was not cinematic.
In the time it takes to draw in one breath she, gone. Not like Liya Kebede,
who runways in Milan, in Johannesburg, in New York, her arms arched and bronze,
as they were when she spun in indigo sky.

The gorge angles in such a way that unless I pitch, like a diver, spelunk,
I'll miss death and encounter something else. That is the risk you take
to elongate splendidly, a spectacle that lasts longer than held breath.
What I need is a boy soldier, a henchman, to catapult, to witness.

COTILLION

The chorine flirts with the mob boss
who splays her atop the white on white
baby grand as the Duke plays "Black and Tan
Fantasy." With each chord she begins to sweat.
Her sugared artistry melts. Her slick updo
meringues into the look for the second shift
at the Savoy. Her beau wears pinstriped
pantaloons. They whirligig the circumference
of the ballroom. The mobster plies her with roses
whose crisp edges curl as brown as her patina.
The photographer waits at the backdoor while
she exits through the front, a borrowed fox draped
askew on her bare shoulders, *I got this in Saratoga*,
he murmurs as he adjusts the glittering eye, *a lucky shot.*

BEAUTY MARK

For Ruby Dee

A gal in rose-colored gingham
Strolls into the officers' mess.
Later, she will wear a black veil
And cry the tears of a crocodile
For a Barbadian bad boy.
I'll not leave her alone the way
He will light out for a scarlet
Hussy in a scoop-neck sheath.
The picnic basket packed
With Mother's fried chicken &
Biscuits left behind on a bench.
Face it honey: a coloratura can't
Compete with a mezzo.
 Bait your hook
 For fish you can fry
No one pays to hear an angel sing.

EGYPTLAND

After Lillian Evanti

In Prague the opera boxes are made of marzipan—
Gilt roses and dainty violets ornament each row.
The prima donna pirouetting on stage does not dizzy.
I am spotting my sisters: Black Patti, the Colored
Coloratura, the Sepia Spinto, and the Mulatta Mezzo.
If I forget the Italian, if I can't grasp high C,
They will sing the chorus as I raise a song
That leads Aïda across Babylonian sands
To the honeyed halls of the Metropolitan.
In the diva's dressing room on an ivory vanity
Velvet gloves wait for me to slip.

In the suite at the Four Seasons, I keep them on, lace fingers
Around his neck, *conduct me*, I whisper into the drum
Of his ear. A bellboy ushers me through the kitchen,
Smiles, apologetic-like, asks for my autograph.

My bosom heaves,
Tortured curls unravel
Into a smoky tiara.
I am a waterfall.
The orchestra drowns.
Still, they strike up a march.

Red gloves sign their own music.
I hold the top note for an eight count.
I can't leave the stage.
If I do, a balcony awaits my leap.
I want to eat with the chorus
Not the Pullman porters.

The gloves are on the stage.
I draw my fingers through
One digit at a time. They fit.
Tight as my gown, heavy silk

Drenched. Some epic.
The curtain calls. A thousand
Roses hurled from heights
Target my neck. Their thorns
Trace a collar of rubies as I scoop
The rainbow mélange
Floral excrement stains the ivory satin.
I leave them for the laundress.

Rosina sung by a girl from the slums
That ragged edge takes the pearl
Sheen off her voice. Watch her scat
In a golden gown. How resplendent
Brünhilde's braids, her Viking victory.
The gloves on the vanity are pristine.
Like my high C. A pureblack sound
They say emanates from my cheekbones.
They pinion my Delilah between pillars.

To make me Bess they paint metallic blue on my skin.
I am so petite. A new wardrobe must be conceived.
I feel naked when Crown takes me in his hot hands
As vulnerable as if I am singing Wagner in a slip.

Tell the glover remake them in black leather.
In this bodice, I dominate the stage dons.
My skin is the costume.
Catch this rose.

The gloves are on the table.
You are first chair tonight.
Extend a hand.

VOICE IS NOT MY INSTRUMENT

when i tell him it was miles said i could sit in
they think i'm jiving. those who do believe
chuckle, pinch my brassy cheeks, presume.
i cut my good hair so it don't detract from my lips
around the horn. horn my daddy thought he'd
learn his son on but he didn't have no son.
valaida say *just cause you can blow better*
than most cats don't mean you not
eye candy for the front of the stage.
i don't scat or croon to their melodies.
ain't a bit jealous of billie's rough mouth
or ivie's canary pitch. (she's the *real* Lady.)
men want to know but it's the women who ask
who i fucked for this seat. the truth:
i'd pay any tithe to swing here.

WILD MAN

A rogue wind carries a luminescent feather
& drums wake the womb. The queen preens
as he calls to the spyboy, feels
his calloused ovals finger braille
on the pelvic floor, *da dum*, whistle
whisper, *you my redbone*, the prettiest.

BEADWORK

A fast hand does not make a masterful stitch.
In his father's, the needle pulls up, then down,
to the teeth, snap. The thread sweeps
a thimble full of blue lotus, begins the rosette.
Who taught these men women's work?
Hands raw from the oyster boats, lips wet
from wild rye. Not your mother. Not she
who never learned to cross-stitch or iron,
who fills pork casings as he gathers the tiniest feathers
& extracts a single, white, pearl from iridescent mayhem,
who fries boudin in cast iron as he chants the long strut
that is St. Joseph's Night.

CAMEO

The witch is going to die, you say, and I know that's right—
shawshanked and stupefied they appear with uncanny
timing, in front of the snowplow after you bogey the 17th,
to swallow a swarm of bees from a consumptive blonde's
fever-stained lips. I mistook her caul for revelation.
Where is Angelique's fairy godsister?
Morbidly obese at 10, she needs more than a pumpkin.
Prince's lean hunger leaps out of huge, lashed eyes.
He sure needs to rub a magical Negro out of his flashlight.
Maybe that's why the most maniacal magicker is that trickster,
Shine, when they begged, borrowed, and bullied, save poor me,
he let them sink.

OUR ARIEL

For Rihanna

Riffing on Marley and sipping coconut water
she finally resembles the beautiful-ugly bajan
babe I knew was she. SKA-AND-DA-LUST...
with a gun? Ina waterfall? A vengeful, flame-haired
Lasiren. Her eyes promise carnival but my Nana
warn me, these Caribbean gals, they will cut she.

NIGHTMARE CHRONICLES

Must be a body sweet on Monk
who gives name to the refrain.
Project-heralds echo the latest:
Pandemic!
Fashion victims fall prey
to street philosophy.

Nightmare logic bleeds into daytime drama.
There is a code to street conduct.
A way to do things that keeps faith
with the shadows still standing
on these corners calling...

Women live among them like oracles
bewitched Cassandras speaking only in rhyme.
They counsel closely, waiting for their Paris.
Only a sociopath works this hard.
What the children whisper:
he has no navel, but many names.
Can't pull my eyes from the entrails
the playful pleasure, a somnambulist's poison.
It's like being fucked in a coma.
Every sense is dumb, but your mind knows
these men, our boys, treasure
maps in hand, searching
each stash of dreams stolen
by everyone with a stake.

LADY WITH A LAMPPOST

And it is her legs
strikingly slung
black and tan fantasy
crossed at the heel
in brand new pumps

that remind me the under-armor of womankind has no traction with my generation.
We go: un-hosed, sans girdle, comfortably free. We like risky business.

A May 1957 issue of *Ebony* lies on an antique vanity—
the afternoon remains of an estate sale.
I imagine it laden with an arsenal of
glass bottles, brushes, and other feminine poisons
designed for appeal, like Hilda Simms,
pinned-up on a lamppost in Harlem,
her hair waves winsome, shellacked
as her cheesecake smile, a tea-length skirt
grazing her knees. I want to rip the cover,
tape it to the oval mirror.

Legs that pretty
and twisted,
in hose (nylons)
once found at Penney's:
10 for a dime.

IN COMMEMORATION OF CONVALESCENCE

Swan your neck & you might glimpse
my tattoo dancing a Creole rhapsody.
The insignia of the House of Bourbon
upside down & inked so green it's algae.
Black jade against the fawn silk betwixt
my slack shoulder blades.
For so long I feared permanence:
the branding of flesh. Then, I played
five-card draw with a dazzle of dolphin kings.
Their sonorous lure led me to their
deep sea table. Four queens and a spade,
when your fingers find the tar stamp
you wish turpentine could lift
from my back the proof
I am no different from other
marked women, what did I win?

HAG-RIDDEN

Our neighbor salts his driveway
Glaring across the street as if
He has X-ray vision and can see
My purple thong, which he is certain
I wear only to spite him.

He is an insomniac asthmatic.
Once an ambulance carried him away
From the zinnias he was planting in July.
The wind caught the seeds as he fell.
By September every house on the block
Had at least one giant bloom.

He plows with a bottle of gin
In his back pocket, pulls the cord of his
Machine and curses at my husband
Who retrieves the paper, but won't
Shovel: "They are killing us softly."

He scratches his neck like a dope fiend
And tugs at his sleeve to reveal bruises.
I pretend to water the hardy mums
But still see the blue-gray fingerprints
Like fairy pinches on a baby's bottom
Numerous as freckles on a redheaded girl.

Past midnight, I let the curtain fall.
He keeps his light on and so I wait
Until I'm sure he has given up
To slip off my skin.
It is a great game this trick I learned
Like everything else in a book borrowed
From the library. No wonder they
Wish to track what we read these days.

Any woman can do this: slide from her flesh
And fly from one roof to the next.
Shimmy like Santa into the flames and kick
Ashes from her heels onto the carpet.

The suburbs are full of lonely men struggling
To stay awake. Our neighbor also reads and has divined
A way to stop my wanderlust, steal the tokens
For my nightly carousel, but my husband sleeps too soundly
Never notices he twirls his fingers in dead hair.

THE DICTATOR'S WIFE, OR MILDRED ARISTIDE PREPARES
TO ADDRESS THE CONGRESSIONAL BLACK CAUCUS

Visionaries seldom find respite
in safe harbors of flesh and bone.
One eye ever cracked on the dream.
Their right hand chokes Damocles' sword.
You are the woman who sleeps beside
clever plotting practice.

Learn to pack light, a small overnight case, practice
abandoning all you cherish with one hour's respite.
What Yankees call carpet bags suffice. Besides,
you've learned to sleep in jewels welded with bone.
One can never be sure what time swords
might cross in front of the *Banque Nationale.* Dream

of Mussolini's mistress, they hung her dream
next to him. Execution requires no forethought, just practice.
Elections seldom cast the same bright aura of destiny's sword.
And so, myths. For myths, one always needs a woman's respite.
Even if American born, she will save the last meat from the bone,
will always add perishables to her valise. Besides,

you can never be sure if your place of exile will be beside
a resort or a prison. Some refuse escort, cling to their dream
of benign oligarchy, literacy, water purification, tourism, bone
china, a U.N. seat, immunizations, and a newly quilted flag. Practice
nationalism at Cabral's heels, recite Che's chants, remember respite:
a feminine touch discourages the people from taking up swords.

Dress for carnival. Make all men believe they might reign, sword
in hand. Do not be too beautiful. Women must identify: *besides
myself who would be a better hostess for affairs of state,* and a respite
for children, who are useful, but more often dangerous dreams.
After all, a child could inherit your carefully nurtured practice
hence ending a need for all elections. Some might have a bone

to pick, but imagine the library portraits set in herring-bone
frames, your descendants finding grandfather's sword
in the palace gardens where your personal militia practices.
Think how they will follow the heroic light beside
your son, if you have a son. If you do not, prepare to dream
another woman might steal your place as his respite.

For now, find respite in your bone
temple, dream of Winnie's words
beside your own and above all, practice.

RESIDUAL

After Kara Walker

Between our skins,
ink and paste, how
to loose the deep desires:
first finger the terrain of scars,
then prick the tempest of
my longing (the whip)
your need to wield it.

THE SEDITIOUS SAGA OF ANNABELLE X AS TOLD TO THE ABOLITIONIST MRS. SARABETH CLARKE OF ROCHESTER, NEW YORK, IN NINE PARTS

THE MEET AWFUL

The closet was the only shelter that came to her. Her instinct to run proved correct. As soon as she softly caught the door closed a shot rang out that rattled the hinges. A stampede: heavy tread spread through the rooms above. Annabelle dropped the basket of peaches. They bruised against her feet & disappeared among the preserve jars & flour sacks on the pantry floor. She did not realize she was praying until the door flew open. His face, his breath, his bottle-green eyes inches from hers. It would constantly surprise, how such a small man could wield such power. Such prowess. Napoleon, she would learn, was one of his idols. His library bulged with biographies of the man, his wives, & his campaigns. In unguarded moments he would call her *his* Josephine. In this moment, all that was before them was unknown. He makes no move without forethought & clear purpose, she relates: he did not hesitate, simply closed the distance between their lips & shut the door. She forgot her voice. Her ignorance—innocence?— was so great that she knew not what he did until it was done. Indeed, says Mrs. Clarke, true women do not suffer such indignities.

ANNABELLE

We are not so different you and I. Like you
I was taken ignorant from my father's house.
Forced into congress with a man not of my choosing
who purchased, nay stole, me for a singular purpose.
I must admit I have experienced real pleasure
such that I knew in my heart I must be as wanton
as a skinned grape, pliant beneath its dark, sour shield.
He is skilled at pulling from me such feelings.
After dispensing painfully with a treasure
useless to the enslaved thus, we began an education.
In his library, I could decipher a life of my own.

THE FINE PRINT

It hurt to ride, afterwards.
So disoriented.
Bode's groom held her on his horse
the long ride to Greyhaven.
Words continued to elude,
yet she did brandish the papers
she always had upon her like a fan.
Bode snatched at a trot the piece of parchment.
Read with his lips, the way a child would,
what she had written herself:

This girl answering to Annabelle belongs to the Beaulieu plantation.
She must be allowed to pass unmolested and returned. Any harm upon
her person will be considered a particular affront as she is my beloved property.
Mr. Harold Worthington.

A stroke of luck. Wouldn't you say, Rod? Massa?
Finding a runaway at Stokes'.
You might say it made an unpleasant trip worthwhile.
Bode laughed and the men in the posse (not Stokes) with him.
He tilted her chin with a single, gloved finger; Annabelle witnessed
her father use the same gesture when he perused merchandise
in the Market while she stood beneath a sunshade, her bottom
lip dropped of its own accord. You can tell the age, he said, by the teeth.
They didn't slow until they reached her new home, not even to put
a bullet in Stokes, whose peaches she had left behind.

DUEL

Word spread like cottonseed.
What Annabelle remembered:
a tray of sweet biscuits & apple butter
untouched in her hands.
I want satisfaction.
Bode had offered Worthington a fortune
(her father was known for his love of dice & dog fights)
still drunk on honor he persevered.
The men came in from the Field.
The white & the black
weighing the skills of the man they knew
over the righteous anger of the one they didn't.
The women, the white & the black
& the not so black, were bemused
to a one by this man who lived open
with his concubine & set free his progeny
in their eighteenth year.
Annabelle was one week shy of freedom.
She was no fugitive.
The odds were not in his favor.

CHIVALRY

I am not what you call a lucky shot.
I don't leave much to chance.
I practice. Let the geese lie where they fall
To remind there is beauty in precision.
It is my way to take what I find
At its value.
Worthington was an honorable man
Worth the bullet.
I let him lay where he fell
To remind Annabelle of the cost
Of her honor.

PEALS OF BELL-SHAPED LAUGHTER

Come live with me free my love
And we will the wine of liberty drink.
Annabelle misquoted words from a stolen book
Of verse but they fell upon deaf ears in Philadelphia.

Bode often forgot the groom Roderick
In his musings upon trade & politics & chattel.
He let her alone and the two fell together much
On the road to Philadelphia.

At night he slept in the stables, but when Bode left
Her bedside he crept in and whispered what the free men
Had told him: on this soil you have only to declare yourself
And it will be so in Philadelphia.

Roderick was Angolan, a prince of the Market.
She had seen his price in Master Bode's book.
One did not need to figure to know he would sell her
Before he let loose his Rod. No one knew horseflesh like he
Who was allowed to carry the cat-o'-nine furled like a rattler at his hip.
She did not trust a man so dark so close to white
But in the kitchen, a free cook validated all he said.
So market day in front of Independence Hall
She went her way and he went his
In Philadelphia.

MASTER BODE

This is an instrument your privileged status has kept from you but that most of your kind have known from birth. Reared from childhood in comfort like any white lady you have had your father's protection and mine. Your actions today have shown you both ungrateful and undeserving of the place I have granted you. Know you will have another place more befitting to your true status—the Field. As for your initiation, the cat-o'-nine will rid you of any lasting pretensions and it will free me from any shreds of affection for your flesh.

I am dedicated in this course and no protest you can offer will deter me.

PLEADING THE BELLY

Bode lowered, but did not drop, the whip.
I should beat it from you.
Then, in a lower register,
Is it mine?

NOSTALGIA

What I like best about Montreal
Is no one speaks English with that
Rugged Kentucky twang. A rancher's
Life is not hard by comparison though
I understand none of the musical
Language everyone sings around me
Including Annabelle, who has learned
Much from working in the kitchens
Of the *Quebecois Hotel*.
She feeds our son toast soaked
In strawberry milk and leaves
Him napping in a hammock strung
Beneath a silver maple far
From the heat of the stoves.
Better is that I can fire my rifle
If someone questions what is mine.
Here I have honor upheld by the law.

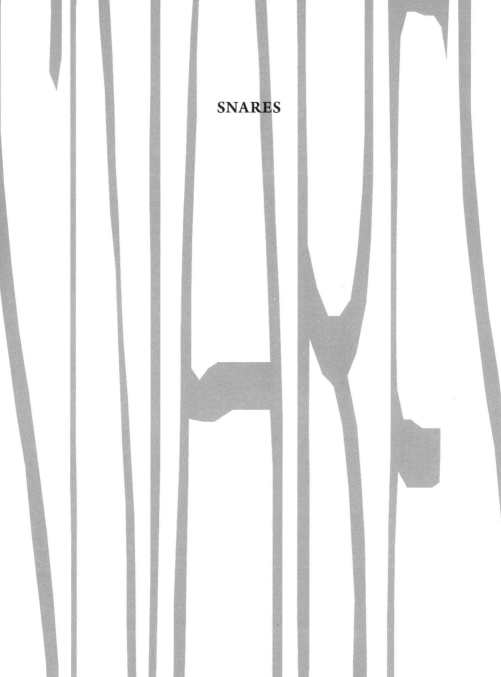

SNARES

THE HOLY CATHEDRAL AT TOLEDO AS PRAISE SHACK

Imagine a shout held in its main gallery.
Voices, like pipe organs to the gothic arches,
caress the treasury, use the gold plates and
scepters as noisemakers to keep the rhythm.

The praise shack on Daufuskie would fit in the bishop's crypt,
an outhouse for the holy spirit rather than a stronghold of
Christendom that marshaled every man with a chisel
to raise pulleys until the inside resembled a heaven
where hosts of marble seraphim backstroke across the ceiling.

The spirit rumbles through the holy hut, sweat and stink
of human humility seep through the floorboards attracting
every flying, flagellating insect in the dark woods
to its frail, inebriated radiance.

The praise shack faces no armory or house of justice.
Its only neighbor a cabin with shutters painted heben blue.
Not fatal, leeched indigo, but the cobalt of Madonna's mantle.
Perhaps the carpenter first saw that blue from the deck of a slave ship?
A blue so blue it fixed them to the shore.

ZORAYA'S LAMENT

Do not let Cypress
roots drag me beneath starrèd
tiles and ringing founts.
There, the sultan's architect
has mortared my lover's blood.

WEEP LIKE A WOMAN FOR WHAT YOU COULD NOT HOLD AS A MAN

Boabdil's mother tells him
as he leaves Alhambra in defeat.
The Court of the Crepe Myrtles
has such a lovely sound to it,
I decide to stay here: a statue
in a geometric garden: one
of a dozen streams of water
strumming the reflection pool;
a carp flipping in a murky fountain;
a duck dozing in red dust; a row
of rose vines arboring a tiled path of teal
and terracotta; one triangle holding
a thousand stars arranged for pretty
rather than use.

FORBID ROSEMARY

Oranges frame entry
to the Mezquita where a
gypsy woman begs.
I snatch her offering—alms
from my husband's open hand.

OUR LADY OF THE ORANGE TREES

To be in a nation unburdened by freedom,
where women have hair darker than mine;

to find tranquility behind a mantilla of silver
shielding eyes of ochre, innumerable browns

that render light irises transparent
is as fresh as a shot from a fallen orange.

When did the women who lay in luxuriant repose
in Alhambra's navel become black-swathed ghosts?

How could a poet write an elegy for desert beauty
if he never looked upon the face of his lover?

In Toledo, bars bisect a golden Madonna;
prison is another form of worship.

WHITE CITY

Córdoba's secret
pristine balconies weep vines
of bougainvillea.
Purple veils hide hennaed hands.
Red tea runs from golden lamps.

IRUÑA

His inane request flatters the Aframericana
riveted by the contrast of Basque-bay eyes
set in dark skin. He has studied her hunger
for conversation in this city of touch
where men tempt her son with marzipan.
The little prince slips from her grasp
charmed by a puppeteer's last act on the plaza.
As siesta descends over the bars and cafes
her inquisitor turns cold. She does not know—
where is the bus station—everything she has
is open to gypsy magic. The Roma and his shadow
demur then salute the little prince as he runs
into arms blushed warm plum.

CASTLE OF OLIVES

Afar, they waver
in bare terrain. Such verdant
sheep, their wool shivers
against the dusk-born breezes
bearing fruit out of our hands.

SEEKING: MUST LOVE SIDEWALK CHALK

After Mary Poppins (1964)

2/3rds in there's a minstrel show,
unexpected, and yet it's impossible
to resist steppin' time: fetch an umbrella
& cakewalk London's aeries, crowing children
from their beds for a midnight carnival.
Awake every hour on the hour, I consider
other mothers: hire a night nurse, they advise,
a spoonful of sugar will help you forget
how she squeezed between the bodies of men,
her darlings left tucked tamale-tight, fingernails
clawing at slivers of air. How fanciful to imagine
her skirts swelling in a warm wind over your border.

LOOK AWAY!

1962 is ancient for the ramshackle cottage nestled between stuccoed condos
& hedged estates. Live Oak: the last street with homes built from real wood.
Once, a quick claimed shantytown for retired hippies who patched tin walls
with surfer's wax & hung homespun afghans against offshore chill. Unlike
those predawn wave-riders, we seldom emerge before noon, wait until the
sun has defeated the gumbo of cloud, fog & mist shrouding the coast, coaxing
the redwoods to suicidal heights. The path through the rocky bluffs to the
sand steeps over pine-straw & dune-debris. I lift our youngest over a hillside
cleft where stashed remnants of a bonfire still smolder, fragrantly. It is only
after I recline beneath the bright jade canopy & we have laid out our picnic
that I see it, convulsing rapidly from a military height above a large, vacant
lot atop bluffs strewn with skeletons of motorbikes & vintage cars. Who it
belongs to is anyone's guess. The converted RV that abuts the lot is a likely
candidate: an eyesore interrupting the view of the spanking-new Queen
Anne on its leeward side. Our leisure is conspicuous, but no one gestures or
yells from the heights. Not the mother, with her blond dreads & naked band
of sanded toddlers, nor the teenagers burrowing each other to their necks.
Our host smiles, apologetic, she sees me see the confederacy's rebirth, welcome
in the midst of liberalism. The sight emboldens. Although I am tomato to
her banana, I squeeze into a proffered wetsuit & paddleboard out on low
tide. Astride, a pod of dolphins nudge my leg, seal-frolic splashes my face &
in the distance a migrating humpback salutes a geyser-blast. Getting up the
gumption to stand takes time. I balance the oversize paddle off center & rise
from a plié when I see it whip to its full length, a bloodied banner bisected by
deep-blue hate. I fall in B & W, a Gus pursued by a Flora, into glacial surf.

EXTRAVAGANT COLORS NOT FOUND IN NATURE

Opaline feels like it sounds
The milky blue of phlegm
A pasty, gluish white
You hope never to discover
On your shoe or shoulder.

Granita is not a sexy drink
But a hard black pounding
In the small of your back
Raising a welt that turns
Ambergris in the sun
And cool cobalt in the shade.

Xerxus: a mercurochromatic red.
The blood you never see in movies
Or transfusions. The last drops
That pump from a battered heart.

When we live only inside the machine
Of the body, cut loose from splendor
Shrunk inside ventricles we will
Know ourselves only by our wizarding ways.
How we found the earth unfinished
And finished it.

SUSTAINABILITY

Our neighbors inform us they have applied for a license to raise chickens.
I tell them my grandmother grew collards between stalks of sugarcane.
Everyone cultivated something on 28th Street. They parked Cadillacs on
Roughdry lawns to make way for the corn and cucumbers lining the drive.
Roosters strutted the stoops. Children cupped hands to catch avocadoes
That rivaled grapefruit before they busted on the sharp, green crabgrass.
The new coop will not prevent grazing on our side of the unfenced yard.
What will happen to my floral ambitions? We recycle. We endure: coffee-
ground compost, rain gardens, solar ovens, electric mowers & water barrels.
I can tolerate the hunger of hares, thieving squirrels & rabid raccoons
But yardbirds pecking at my daylilies is too much like what I left behind:
Laundry on the line and foulness of fowl strung by their toes, drying,
Then shorn, then fried.

COVENANT

I tell you the story of the witch and the Indian who came first with his story of the frog that swallowed the world & gave birth to the witch. Her hair was as long as the last night of the year when she opened her mouth to take her first breath Spider crawled out a tambourine in each eight. This raucous arachnid spun a web of music that shimmered into the universe. The witch's delight was terrible to behold so the Indian enslaved her to stop her laughter, start her loving him & his people as her own people. She brought: bison & corn, rain & earth that trembled. The Indian thought that he was safe as long as the witch loved him but one day she heard the croaking of a frog & abandoned her children. The Indian sent his best arrows after her but forgot she knew how to ride the air, her children, however, could not. In their grief they hunted the bison and ravaged the corn. O say can you see her dancing to Spider's song on the shortest day.

WHAT WE KNOW AS PRISTINE

My youngest turns his left eye,
as limpid and lazy as this black pond
flanked by golden grass
behind which row upon row
of ash, maple, and cottonwood
shimmer silvered medallions
of green that cast no reflection
as dragonflies murmur
a path through the grass to
their favorite skimming site,
west of where I have abandoned
labor in full sun as distracted by
serene vistas as by his peripheral gaze.

COOKING WITH GLASS

"My purpose in life is making you a good dinner."
—Ina Garten

My son's kindergarten eats kohlrabi for snack.
Cool Rabbi—he enunciates—is yummy with ranch.
The science of food is like the alchemy of love.
Too much tinkering ruins what is best simply solo.

Consider the blood orange:
its sinful interior is all the rage.
Now, it's a sidecar or marmalade—
a vampire's amuse-bouche.

Adding saffron to everything is so precious
I haggled over a thimble of threads in Marrakech.
Now, Costco shelves pounds of pulverized gold
as ubiquitous as sundried tomatoes,
which catch between my teeth, in quiche.

A waitress extols: it's the new bacon.
The hot chocolate, she confides,
is ninety-nine percent pure.

I ask for a straw.

BETWEEN PICKLED PEARS AND PRESERVED PEACHES I FIND

A spell to summon dragons
A charm to vanquish ghosts
A potion to alleviate ill luck
A talisman to keep away demons
A chant to call an angel
A cloak that renders you visible
An umbrella that hides your pores
Boots that let you cross against the light
Boots that keep you wet on dry land
A car that flies
A carpet that lies
A tune to conjure cats
Another to send them back
What my mother does for cramps
Mix seven parts with one part
Honey makes it go down easy
What to leave for the dead
What to leave for children
How to catch a fox
How to tame a doctor
When to fish or cut bait
When to shush or blow your top
When to shame the devil
When to kiss a frog
How to be a saint
How to be a dancing queen
A mojo to banish the boogie
What I know for sure
Leave lipstick on your cup
It will bring you home

BLOOD-RED VELVET WITH SCREAM PLEASE, FROST ME

Her dream is a storefront sanctified by sugar
Where Gayma's signature 7UP cake sparkles
Amidst loaves of lard-lathered bread shadowed
By cinnamon. Maybe an espresso, a tisane to wash
Rhubarb-apple crisp from your bruised, honeyed lips.
Babygirl, don't hurt yourself running after these fine
Chocolate macaroons. The ones studded with golden
Walnuts and shaved coconut. Might as well call them
Zulu cakes: one bite works deadly upon the tongue.

ACKNOWLEDGMENTS

My thanks to the editors of the following publications in which these poems first appeared:

Prairie Schooner: "Blood-Red Velvet with Scream Please, Frost Me"

Los Angeles Review: "The Holy Cathedral at Toledo as Praise Shack"

Tidal Basin Review: "One Moment She was There and the Next" and "Lady with a Lamppost"

Crab Orchard Review: "The Dictator's Wife, or Mildred Aristide Prepares to Address the Congressional Black Caucus"

The Ringing Ear: Black Poets Lean South: "Residual"

Obsidian vol. 43.2: "Cotillion" and "Look Away!"

I lift up in gratitude the community of friends, family, and fellow poets whose fingerprints are all over these pages. For space and sustenance: I thank my colleagues at the University of Wisconsin-Madison, the fellows and faculty of Cave Canem (past, present, and future), and the staff and fellow residents at Vermont Studio Center and the Ragdale Foundation. For love and laughter: my sons, and as always, Amaud.

CHERENE SHERRARD was born in Los Angeles. A Cave Canem Graduate Fellow, she is the author of the chapbook, *Mistress, Reclining*, winner of the New Women's Voices Award, and a biography of Harlem Renaissance writer Dorothy West. Her poems have appeared in the *Los Angeles Review, Crab Orchard Review, Prairie Schooner*, and *Tidal Basin Review*. She is the recipient of a Wisconsin Arts Board Grant in poetry, a National Endowment for the Humanities Award, and a resident fellowship from the Ragdale Foundation. She currently lives in Wisconsin, where she is a professor in the English department at UW-Madison.

St. Francis and the Flies by **Brian Swann**
WINNER OF THE 2015 AUTUMN HOUSE POETRY PRIZE
Selected by Dorianne Laux

Bull and Other Stories by **Kathy Anderson**
WINNER OF THE 2015 AUTUMN HOUSE FICTION PRIZE
Selected by Sharon Dilworth

Presentimiento: A Life in Dreams by **Harrison Candelaria Fletcher**
WINNER OF THE 2015 AUTUMN HOUSE NONFICTION PRIZE
Selected by Dinty W. Moore

Glass Harvest by **Amie Whittemore**

Apocalypse Mix by **Jane Satterfield**
WINNER OF THE 2016 AUTUMN HOUSE POETRY PRIZE
Selected by David St. John

Heavy Metal by **Andrew Bourelle**
WINNER OF THE 2016 AUTUMN HOUSE FICTION PRIZE
Selected by William Lychack

RUN SCREAM UNBURY SAVE by **Katherine McCord**
WINNER OF THE 2016 AUTUMN HOUSE NONFICTION PRIZE
Selected by Michael Martone

The Moon is Almost Full by **Chana Bloch**

Vixen by **Cherene Sherrard**

The Drowning Boy's Guide to Water by **Cameron Barnett**
WINNER OF THE 2017 RISING WRITER PRIZE
Selected by Ada Limón

For our full catalog please visit: http://www.autumnhouse.org

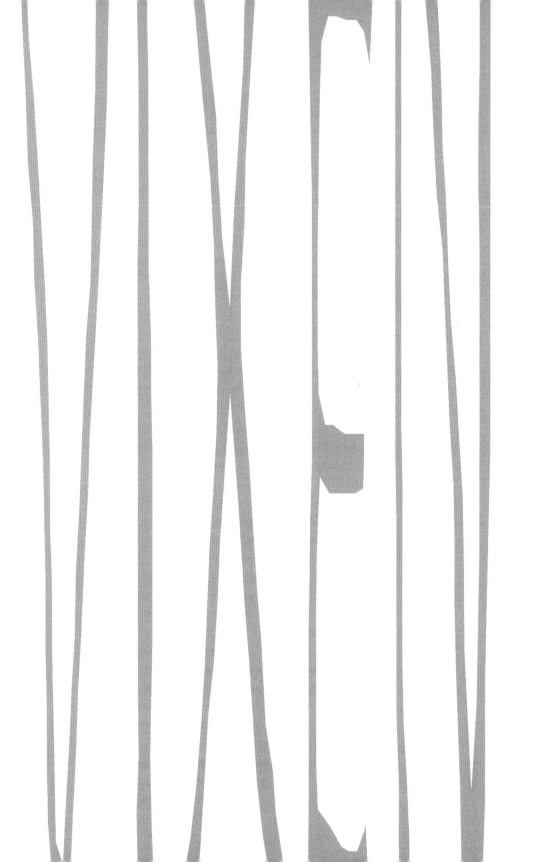